HOW TO BORROW AND LOAN KINDLE BOOKS IN JUST 30 SECONDS

LOAN BOOKS FROM PUBLIC LIBRARIES WITH UPDATED STEP BY STEP GUIDE WITH SCREENSHOTS FOR ALL DEVICES WITH TIPS & TRICKS

Mac Andrews

TABLE OF CONTENTS

COPYRIGHT..2

TABLE OF CONTENTS 3

10 KEY POINTS TO TAKE NOTE OF 4

HOW TO LOAN BOOKS FROM KINDLE OWNERS' LENDING LIBRARY 6

HOW TO ACCEPT LOAN 11

HOW TO BORROW A KINDLE BOOK FROM A KINDLE READER 14

HOW TO BORROW A BOOK FROM KINDLE FIRE ..17

HOW TO BORROW A KINDLE BOOK FROM PUBLIC LIBRARIES USING AN OVERDRIVE 20

HOW TO SHARE BOOKS ON AMAZON HOUSEHOLD FROM THE AMAZON FAMILY 22

How to Share All Your Content: 24

SOME EXTRA TIPS 25

CONCLUSION 27

10 KEY POINTS TO TAKE NOTE OF

Here are the 10 things you should put into consideration first before you learn how to borrow and loan Kindle Books:

1.   A borrower cannot accept a book loan if such book is unavailable in the his/her country.

2.   If you get the loan, you must accept it within 7 days.

3.   Some Kindle books are not lendable.

4.   The notes and highlights you make on your book will not be visible to any one you loan out your book to.

5.   You can borrow two or more books to your Household Library and Amazon Family members.

6.   You can neither access a kindle books that is on loan nor read it.

7.   You can only borrow a particular book once, unless you intend to share it with family members using Amazon Family.

8.   You can only use kindle devices to read books from Kindle Owners' Lending Library, while other   devices   as   well   as   Kindle   reading

applications can be used to read Kindle Unlimited books.

9.   You cannot borrow a Kindle book for more than 14 days.

10.   You cannot share magazines and papers.

Now that we have the 10 key points to note before you begin the guide, it is time to learn the steps on lending books using the Kindle Owners' Lending Library.

HOW TO LOAN BOOKS FROM KINDLE OWNERS' LENDING LIBRARY

Most Kindle users do not know about the Kindle Owners' Lending Library (KOLL). Also, they are unaware that KOLL has up to 2 million available titles. If you follow these steps, you can lend a Kindle book from KOLL in about 30 seconds:

#1: Go to your account on www.amazon.com. Click on Your Digital Content & Devices. You can either go straight to www.amazon.com/mycd or Log in using your email and password.

#2: Check the list of Your Content for the book.

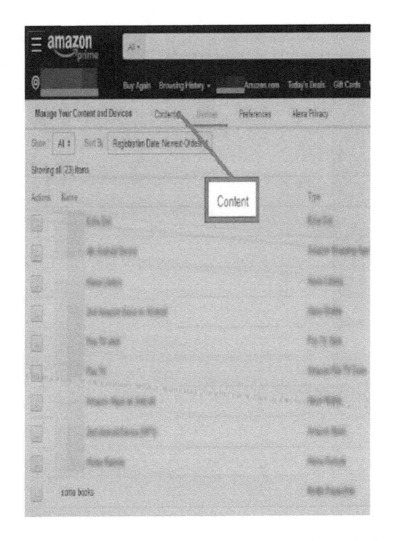

#3: At the book's left, you will see a three-dash icon. Click on it.

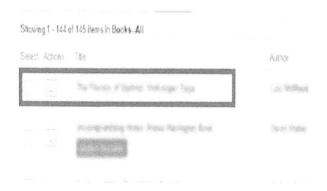

#4: A window will pop up. Click Loan this Title on it.

> Deliver to my...
> Download & transfer via USB
> Clear furthest page read...
> Delete from library
> Manage Kindle FreeTime Content
> Loan this title

#5: Complete the loan by filling the blank spaces.

I.   Recipient's Email Address: The e-mail address of your friend

II.   Recipient's Name: The name of your friend

III.   From: Your e-mail address

IV. Personal Message: Here, you may include a personal message

#6: Click on the Send Now button.

Yay! You have successfully loaned your friend a Kindle book in 30 seconds. Your friend will get an email to this effect in a couple of minutes. You may have to remind your friend to accept the loan within 7 days.

Note: If you do not get this loan option, it means the book is not loanable.

HOW TO ACCEPT LOAN

If you want to read a book that is sent to you, you first have to accept it. After receiving the Amazon email of acceptance with a subject like "A Loaned Book for You", you should follow these 5 easy steps:

#1: Open the Loan Confirmation Mail sent by Amazon.

#2: Click on the Get your loaned book now button.

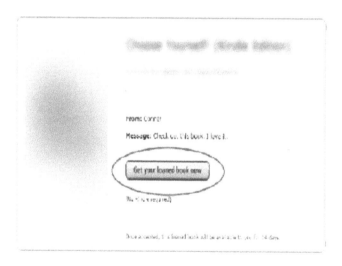

#3: To continue, Log in to your Amazon account.

#4: When you see the accept loan page, click on Choose your device in the green square box.

#5: Click the Accept loaned book button.

Go ahead and read your book on your Kindle apps in any device.

HOW TO BORROW A KINDLE BOOK FROM A KINDLE READER

The process of using your Kindle device to borrow a Kindle book is quite simple and can be done in just five steps under not more than 30 seconds. Here is the process:

#1: On your Kindle, go to Kindle Store, then click on All Categories.

#2: Click on Kindle Owners' Lending Library.

#3: The book will have a badge of Prime which means that you can go ahead and borrow the title.

#4: Click Borrow for free.

#5: The book will download to your kindle library immediately. You can only borrow one book each calendar month.

HOW TO BORROW A BOOK FROM KINDLE FIRE

You will follow practically the same process when using either a Kindle Tablet or a Kindle Fire. However, some users may not find the process very easy. Here is a step-by-step guide:

#1: On the Kindle Fire, go to Fire Bookstore then find Kindle Owners' Lending Library.

#2: Click the book you intend to borrow.

#3: Check the book to see if there is a badge of Prime on it. If there is one, you can borrow that title.

#4: Click "Borrow for free".

The Kindle book will download automatically into your library, like it does on the Kindle E-Reader. You can borrow one book a month.

HOW TO BORROW A KINDLE BOOK FROM PUBLIC LIBRARIES USING AN OVERDRIVE

Another option you can try for borrowing books is using a public library. This is one of the best options because everyone has a public library in their city. Through this method, you can easily use the books to get them on your Kindle for free.

Most Kindle users are not aware of this method. In order to make use of this method, use your Kindle Fire's Overdrive App or access Overdrive website on www.overdrive.com.

Only U.S. libraries can use Kindle Books Library Loans.

#1: On www.overdrive.com, open the Library's Digital Collection.

#2: Use the "Format Filter" to filter your books, then choose Kindle Books.

#3: Click on the title.

#4: Choose "Borrow Book".

#5: You can now see the book on your Account/Checkouts page.

#6: Click "Read in Kindle".

Read now with kindle

#7: A new Amazon tab will pop up. Click on the "Deliver to" button to check for your device

#8: Click on the "Get Library Book".

Note: The loan expiration date depends on the library you are using.

HOW TO SHARE BOOKS ON AMAZON HOUSEHOLD FROM THE AMAZON FAMILY

Apparently, the methods used above have time limitations. However, there is a way you can lend books with no time limitation. This is possible using a Family Library which is one of the options on Amazon Household. You can either share one book with a member or share an entire library with all the members of this Family Library. Here is how you can do either of these two:

How to Share One Book:

#1: Go to your account on www.amazon.com, then click "Your Digital Content & Devices". You can also go through www.amazon.com/mycd or Log in using your E-mail and password.

#2: Check for your book on the list of Your Content.

#3: At the left side of the book, you will see a "Three-dash icon". Click on it.

#4: A menu will pop up, click Manage Family Library.

#5: Look for the family member you intend to share the book with and next to their name, choose Add to Library.

HOW TO SHARE ALL YOUR CONTENT:

#1: Go to "Manage Your Household"

#2: Click the arrow. You will see the "Manage Your Family Library" button.

#3: Use the "Share Button" to swipe all the items you will like to share under the name of the family member. You can share eBooks as well as other digital content.

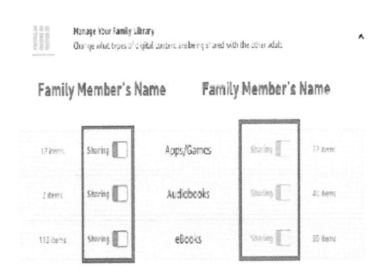

SOME EXTRA TIPS

Save all screenshots

When you tap simultaneously on the bottom right and top left corners or on the bottom left and top right corners, it will take a screenshot of whatever is on your screen at the time, just as you would normally do with your smartphones. A blink will show that you have successfully taken a screenshot. When you connect the device to your computer, you will easily download the images.

Boost autonomy

To extend your Kindle battery's life, you have to activate airplane mode, then go to "Settings" and disable the "Update" page. This will give you some extra time without having to connect to the network.

Delete suggestions

Go to "Settings > Device Options > Advanced Options" and disable the Home Screen. This will make it possible to view only your own collection.

Export highlights and notes

Go to "Settings > Notes > Popular" and find the passages that other users highlighted. To export underlined quotations, click on "Notes" and select

"Export notes". You will receive an Email in .csv and .pdf format.

CONCLUSION

Hopefully, this guide will help you get your favorite Kindle Books. There are lots of Amazon Kindle Unlimited service features that many people do not know yet. This guide will help you get the best out of your Amazon Kindle.